THE ART OF
SCENE
PAINTING

THE ART OF
SCENE
PAINTING

JOHN COLLINS

FOREWORD BY
NICHOLAS GEORGIADIS

HARRAP · LONDON

THE ART OF SCENE PAINTING

FOR BARBARA

First published in Great Britain 1985
by HARRAP LIMITED
19/23 Ludgate Hill, London EC4M 7PD

© *John Collins* 1985

ISBN 0 245-54208-6

Designed by Roger King Graphic Studios
Typeset by Spire Print Services Ltd, Salisbury
Printed and bound in Great Britain
by R. J. Acford, Chichester

Contents

**THE ART OF
SCENE
PAINTING**

Foreword

Almost every theatre designer must have had moments of acute anxiety about the fate of his half-inch model. What will it look like when it is enlarged more than twenty times? The economic realities of the theatre are such as to admit no trial and error. Once the scenery has been made it is very unlikely that anybody would be prepared to pay for another version if the designer finds the interpretation of his work unsatisfactory.

This book presents us with a practical manual of reference, a vocabulary that the designer can use in communicating with the scenic artist. It is the more valuable because it is compiled by an artist of special sensibility, whose position as collaborator with the Old Vic, and later as head of the RSC paint-shop at Stratford, gave him a double advantage over his colleagues. He embodies the nineteenth-century tradition in scene-painting, and when that tradition came into question he had to employ all his considerable ingenuity to finding new solutions to new problems. His acquaintance with such contradictory theories of stage design has forced him to investigate the nature of artistic interpretation, beyond the mere processes of enlargement and slavish copying.

This is a book that will be of equal interest to scenic artist and to stage designer.

Nicholas Georgiadis

Preface

I compiled this manual, or guide to the art of scene-painting, with the thought in mind that a clear, concise and practical guide to the skill was perhaps not readily available; and that I could fill this gap in the market. That is what I have attempted to do, through my words and the illustrations that I have carefully selected. I have attempted to give a thorough analysis — within a relatively small compass — of methods, techniques and materials; and the inherent problems involved in the central problem of the art, which is of enlarging a subject and conveying a visual message to the audience. Since 1946 I have been a scene-painter: at the Old Vic, on my own account, at the RSC at Stratford. Theory has joined with practice, and I am a long-time lecturer at the Slade School. Mine were the Stations of the Cross at St Laurence's Church, Catford; and I was particularly pleased some years ago to paint the murals at the New Festival Theatre, Pitlochry. These murals were painted on either side of the proscenium and the colours of the auditorium seats and walls were in harmony.

If I mention a few odd details of my career in this Preface it is merely to emphasize that my working life has been spent in the service of this great art — an art, moreover, that enjoys a long and illustrious lineage — and that I will count any fragment of skill or particle of enjoyment that can be transmitted to my readers reward in itself.

Introduction

This is a guide to practical work engendered in the bowels of a painter's workshop. The intention is to inform, and the information concerns formulas and recipes for various paints and plasters and other mixtures for the painting and texturing of surfaces. There is also a description of tools, brushes, etc., and notes on the stretching of canvas and the suitability of materials for the task in hand.

Of the artistic value of the end-product little or nothing will be said, as this is of a personal and sometimes fashionable nature, nearly always controversial.

The craft of scenic and architectural painting in tempera colours on canvas is a very old one, in which Canaletto and the Bibienna family were among the greatest exponents; the methods link with the traditional wall-painting of the fourteenth and fifteenth centuries. The careful drawing before painting, sometimes executed on paper and then traced or 'pounced' on to the prepared surface — in fact, the whole scene paint-shop with its frames and movable palettes — seems to echo the old-master artist's studio of the distant past. There are many methods still surviving which may have been invented in Florence or Venice.

The gradual influence of the architect-designer over the painter-designer, and the resulting tendency towards three-dimensional objects rather than painted canvas, is one of the reasons for the change and development of new methods and materials in the paint-shop. Timber, plywood, hardboard, etc., hold sway over canvas stretched on a light-timbered frame (known traditionally as a flat), and consequently paints, dyes and wood stains more suitable for these harder surfaces have come into use, and the surfaces themselves embrace many different textures.

I shall begin with the old methods and pigments and try to show the development through to the present methods.

Workshop and Equipment

The Continental method of painting of scenery on the floor is rarely used in England, because of the large area required, but I shall touch briefly upon this method later. The perpendicular method is most commonly used in this country, and is the one I shall describe.

Canvas is stretched on to a wooden frame which is suspended on four or more wires through pulleys in the roof of the paint-shop, balanced by counterweights and motivated by a hand-winch or electric motor.

The other method is when, through lack of height, the frame is fixed and a bridge is lifted up and down in front.

The first method is the best because the painter has the full space on the shop floor, whereas the bridge is usually very narrow, and everything — paints, brushes, etc. — has to be carried, and the painter is unable to stand back and view the work.

A selection of brushes and fitches, a charcoal stick and a chalk-line.

The RSC scene paint-shop, showing a gas stove with a size-bucket in water.

The average building used by scene-painters is rectangular in shape and can be large enough to hold at least four paint frames, one on each of its long walls and two in the centre, hanging back-to-back. This is more valuable commercially — in the economic use of space — than considering the practical working conditions of the painter and the space needed.

My preference is for the frames hanging side by side that can be used individually, but when required lock together to take larger cloths or cycloramas.

The working floor of the building must be at a level sufficient to allow the full height of the frame above and below; this is sometimes achieved by constructing pits and trenches at ground-level.

The frame travels vertically through a cut in the floor wide enough to take built scenery, yet allow for safety regulations. The paint-shop is a place for professional, adult workers, ever conscious of the need for safe, cautious use of equipment.

There should be an adequate water-supply with large sinks or tanks fitted with filter boxes similar to those used in sculptor's and plasterer's shops, and gas rings with large grills sufficient to carry buckets. A large metal tank a foot deep in which to place buckets in hot (not boiling) water is the best method of heating glue. Sufficient space is required to keep the powder pigments in metal containers with lids, the size depending on the amount to be stored.

Palettes should be of a movable type and not clumsy, but large enough to take about fourteen colours. The type I use is approximately $5' \times 2'6''$ raised on a movable frame to $2'9''$; the height is very important for comfortable working. The colours are mixed to a thick paste in water and arranged around the edge of the palette in containers (plastic basins, boxes, etc.). The centre of the palette should have a smooth white surface impervious to water — e.g., Formica or blockboard with several coats of oil paint rubbed down.

A palette on ball castors for easy movement.

THE ART OF SCENE PAINTING

Among the tools required are straight edges — light-weight strips of wood about 6′ long, bevelled on one side. Compasses should stretch to a minimum radius of 2′6″. A chalk-line is needed, and a charcoal drawing-stick (a bamboo cane fitted with a clip to hold charcoal), also a plumb-line, a ruler, and a flogger (canvas strips fixed to a cane or shaft). Brushes should be of the best bristle (lily-white). Sometimes it is impossible to obtain the larger brushes, which consist of a less expensive bristle, but are capped

Large compasses.

with lily-white. Bristle is still acquired from the boars of northern Russia and China, and for fine work cannot be surpassed. I have experimented with synthetic-fibre brushes but found them lacking in their capacity to hold colour and in spring. The size and type of brush used is again a personal choice.

The art of scene-painting is the understanding of enlarging and of communicating a visual message to the eye of the audience. Any work too small is lost; therefore I always recommended using the largest brush possible for the mark to be made. I rarely use a brush smaller than a No. 8 fitch (about $\frac{3}{4}''$), and a variety of sizes up to No. 14; after that flat brushes from $2''$ to $4''$. Also, sash-tools, varnish brushes, and for the large area lay-in brush; I use the very best bristle, two knot; expensive, but essential in conventional scene-painting. With modern work brushes are sometimes not necessary at all, but if they are it is wiser to use a poorer-quality bristle because of the destructive nature of modern paints and plasters.

Cupboards should be fitted in such a way that bound brushes can be kept suspended by a small hook or loop in the handle; unbound brushes should be suspended in water in order to keep the stock tight. Never wash brushes in hot water, as this causes the bristle to soften and spread. When brushes are not in use for any length of time it is good to dip them in a light size to set the bristle into proper shape. New brushes should be lightly beaten against the hand to rid them of short-cut bristles (trade term, flirting). I will talk more later regarding the holding of a brush, but of course it should be obvious that scrubbing the points of the bristle can only be misuse of a good tool.

Physical Basis of Painting

The physical basis of all painting is essentially similar, regardless of the different processes and materials involved. Basically, a painting is composed of various layers — support, ground-priming, paint layer, protective layer (e.g., varnish or glaze). The material of the support varies according to its purpose. Wood panel, metal, glass, parchment, silk, paper, chipboard, hardboard, linen or leather — there is almost no end to the substances that can be used. In conventional scene-painting the most common material is canvas, but there are also linens and muslins and various kinds of gauze used for transparent and transformation effects. Duck-cloth and sail-cloth are available for strong wear — e.g. stage cloths; while coarse materials such as hessian are used for drapes. With regard to timber, plywood, hardboard, etc., in the old-fashioned painted scene, these were covered with the same material as the rest of the scenery in order to obtain an overall texture.

Traditional scenery is usually comprised of canvas-covered frames known as flats, and soft-canvas rolled on battens, as well as borders and drapes. I shall begin with the treatment of a backcloth made of canvas. This normally arrives from the construction-carpenter, battened top and bottom and rolled on the bottom batten, the size depending on the stage for which it is designed. We will take as an example an average stage, such as the Royal Shakespeare Theatre, which takes a cloth 40' × 26'. The cloth is hung on the top rail of the frame and pinned by about five 4" nails, then carefully unrolled. It is never allowed to drop and unroll itself, as this can tear the cloth and is also rather dangerous because of the possibility of its becoming unpinned. It is allowed to hang free, and when it is hanging plumb the bottom batten is also pinned. Now the sides are tacked out from top to bottom, the tacks spread about 4" apart.

Preparation

There are many ways of preparing or priming canvas, depending on the nature of the painting to follow and the personal taste of the painter. I always prefer soft and pliable cloths which can be folded up, so this is the kind of preparation I shall describe.

A white priming is often used, although if the canvas is sound and white I prefer to give it a coat of size, or flour-paste.

Size
Size is made from glue, and is supplied in many different forms, usually crystals or concentrated powder. It is therefore difficult to make hard-and-fast rules about its use. As good indication of quantities, approximately 1 lb of glue-size makes two to three gallons of strong size. When this thickens it should be of the consistency of a table jelly. This we shall call 'treble size', and it is the strongest mixture of size to be employed (though it is in fact rarely ever used at this strength). To make size, soak the glue-size in cold water, enough to just cover; leave overnight, add boiling water, but do not allow the size to boil.

Priming
Use one part treble size, one part water, and half a part whiting (which is chalk, or calcium carbonate), previously mixed to a thick paste in water. This is a normal priming suitable for tackling cloths and flats, etc., to give the canvas a coat of medium-strength size and to retain the texture of the canvas. The application of the priming should be smooth and fairly quick in order to keep the painting edge wet, and so prevent hard brush-marks appearing. The brush-strokes must be small and in a rhythmic criss-cross pattern, so that in the event of them showing afterwards they make an overall texture.

The Paint Layer

In traditional scene-painting the paint layer is pigment suspended in the medium of glue-size. Aniline dyes, transparent emulsion and spirit varnishes will be dealt with separately.

The use of pigment for decorative purposes is certainly a very ancient art, for much of the material was available in Nature to early man. For white he could use chalk or clays, while charcoal and some dark clays gave him the blacks; and countless yellows and red ochres and greens were present in abundance in the earth.

In the earliest times there was no fixative, and so, unlike carving or metalwork, most early paintings perished (except of course, the cave paintings of primitive man, which were preserved by chance). Egypt, Sumer, Greece, Etruria, Rome, all have remains of fine paintings, for the art of the fresco (applying pigment on to wet plaster) was known 8,000 years BC. The Egyptians were very skilled in the techniques of painting, as can be seen from their wall decorations and the painting on their coffins. They obtained their yellows and reds from the ochre deposits, the blues and greens from the copper ores and other colours from the glazes of the potters. In Greek and Roman frescoes also the earth colours were well known. Earth colours roughly consist of clays which are coloured by the compounds of iron or manganese present in the earth; those rich in iron are the redder, and sometimes the yellows are 'cooked' in order to redden them. Copper ores gave magnificent greens and azures, sulphides gave reds and vermilions.

The use of dyes was well understood, and also the staining of chalk and white clays to make cheaper pigments, blacks from burning bones, gums, fats, dried leaves, etc. These colours were all known in Egypt, and, added to the tints developed by the Greeks and Romans, gave an already embarrassing number of pigments. Exotic colours such as ultramarine (once made from the semi-precious stone lapis lazuli) are a thing of the past, but the important thing to understand regarding pigments is that while some are permanent, others are fugitive.

In my opinion a restricted palette is advisable because a complicated mixture of colours usually cancels out brightness and clarity.

My own list is as follows, starting on the right-hand side of the palette with earth colours.

Yellow Ochre
Raw Umber
Venetian Red
Lemon Chrome
Orange Chrome
Crimson Lake
Light Brunswick Green
Dark Brunswick Green
Blue Lake
Azure Blue
Ultramarine
Drop Black
Whiting (chalk, calcium carbonate)

In addition:

Raw Sienna
Burnt Umber
Indian Red
Leather Lake
Scarlet Lake
Black Lake
Titanium ⎫
Zinc   ⎬   white
      ⎭

I shall give a simple description of the pigments I have mentioned, and a hint as to their best use.

Yellow Ochre. Opaque, and has slightly chalky quality; not suitable for glazes.

Raw Sienna. Opaque; richer and warmer than ochre.

Leather Lake. A very rich, raw sienna, but translucent, a beautiful pigment very suitable for glazes.

Raw Umber. An opaque earth colour, and a rather coarse pigment which if not properly bound tends to rub up. Can also be unpleasantly chalky and a bad mixer.

Burnt Umber. Semi-opaque, and, as its name implies, a richer, warmer brown than raw umber (made by roasting umber).

Venetian Red. Opaque. Pleasant, rich brick-red; very good mixer.

Indian Red. Opaque. Slightly darker and deeper than Venetian Red.

Lemon Chrome. Translucent. A pure colour. Can be made into middle chrome by the addition of orange chrome. A clean mixer.

Orange Chrome. Semi-translucent. A bright but slightly chalky pigment. Tends to muddy a mix.

Crimson Lake. Translucent. Excellent pigment, mixes well, but has no body, and is therefore very suitable for glazes.

Scarlet Lake. Semi-translucent. Can be rather chalky, muddy mixer.

Light Brunswick Green. Semi-translucent, body colour. Good mixer.

Dark Brunswick Green. Translucent. Fine pigment, good mixer.

Blue Lake. (*Cerulean*). Brilliant pigment, good mixer.

Azure Blue. Opaque. Pure, cobalt-like colour, rather chalky.

Ultramarine. Strong opaque.

Drop Black. Good, regular brownish-black, needs extra-strong medium to bind it.

Black Lake. Carbon-blue, purple-black. Semi-translucent.

Whiting (chalk, calcium carbonate). Soft, creamy-white, heavy, opaque.

Titanium White. Intense, opaque.

Zinc White. Intense, but translucent.

Mediums

Size

The fixing of scene-paint powder has until recently depended on glue-size as the fixative. I shall talk about other fixatives later. Glue-size has already been described; the strongest form we call treble size. It is important to understand that the size is used to fix the pigment, and need never be stronger than necessary to stop the colour rubbing. Too strong a size will cause cracking. Four parts water to one part treble should hold an ordinary paint mix; but dilute further, six parts water to one part treble, for glaze-wash work. The dilution must be regular throughout the work, as a change in strength of size can affect the tone and colour of the paint.

Preliminary work to painting a backcloth in size medium on flax canvas. After the cloth has been stretched and primed as described earlier, preparations are made for drawing and painting. The professional scene-painter is mainly employed in copying, or if you wish translating, another man's design. For obvious reasons this is the best starting-point to study scene-painting because of the technical ability needed to enlarge another person's design twenty-four times and not lose the personal quality. When a painter is working from his own design he has more freedom and creative licence, and is not limited by the restriction of copying a $\frac{1}{2}''$ scale-model or drawing. The best scenic work is done when the painter translates the feeling of the work rather than slavishly copying it. In the case of important textural qualities and accidents it is essential that the accident is recreated rather than stiffly copied; this of course requires great control and skill, and is the hallmark of a top scene-painter.

The traditional method of squaring up is mostly used, but it has one great danger — the tendency to execute the drawing in a mechanical way, following the pattern throughout the squares rather than thinking of the form and its living meaning. The scene-painter should merely use the lines as a guide, he should always think of the form of drawing and its meaning. A line is a horizon of form, part

THE ART OF SCENE PAINTING

of a tree, quality of flesh, or stone, or whatever: the painter should not think of a line as placed in a certain square, but always of it as an intelligent indication to the form.

The usual scale in an English paint-shop is $\frac{1}{2}''$ to $1'$. The average size of a stage proscenium opening is between 29'6" (Old Vic, Sadler's Wells, and the Royal Shakespeare Theatre's 30') and the Drury Lane's 40', and even greater. Prosceniums and pelmet border are in proportion to the width. For the purpose of example I shall describe the painting of a backcloth 40' wide by 24' deep, and for subject take the traditional architectural scene, such as one by a member of the Bibienna family.

In order to keep a sense of proportion and maintain a free-flowing line, a charcoal stick about 3' long is employed, as previously described. Scene-painter's charcoal is about $\frac{3}{8}''$ thick, and is supplied in bundles of sticks about 6" in length.

Using the charcoal drawing-stick.

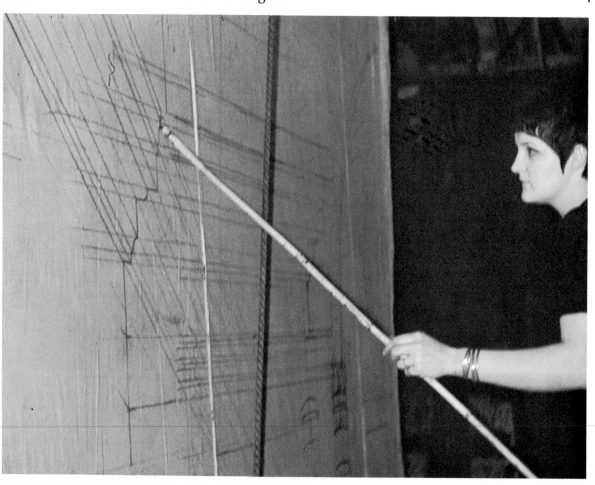

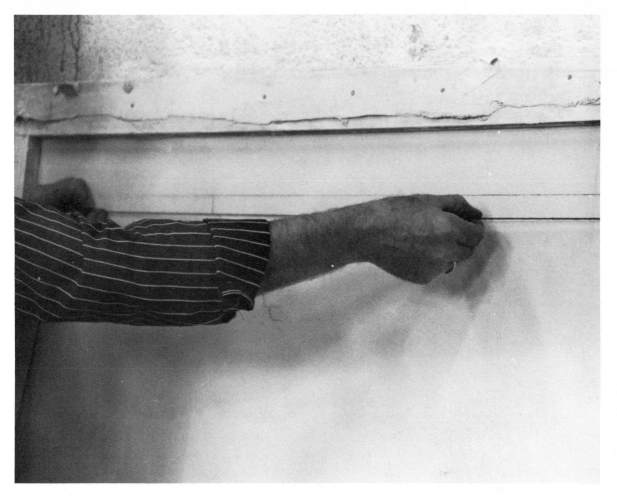

Mark the centre of the cloth at top and bottom, and strike a level base-line. This is done by two people holding each end of a length of string, rubbed in charcoal, through points already marked, and the line is then snapped in the centre, leaving a neat thin line. Having decided the size of the squares (I usually use 3′ squares, though never less than 2′, because they can become confusing), drop a plumb-line from the top centre and strike the centre vertical line. Starting the squares from the base-line up and centre line out, it is best to mark from a straight edge rather than a ruler, as there is less chance of error. The eye must be level with the mark on the straight edge, otherwise it will make an untruthful mark.

When the cloth has been squared up the original drawing must be squared in an identical way in order to have an exact replica. This is best done with a white pencil on a cover of cellophane.

126,647

Snapping a chalk-line.

THE ART OF SCENE PAINTING

Do not be heavy-handed with the charcoal, as the marks are difficult to get rid of. The drawing must be strong yet sensitive; free, yet controlled. The painter has to be aware of the form all the time, and conscious of what he cannot see above his head or beneath his feet. In an architectural scene I draw like a builder, firstly the major foundation points and perspective lines, the great openings, arches, doorways, etc., main cornices, entablature, columns and capital plinths, finishing with the decoration and lesser stuff.

When you have concluded a satisfactory drawing in charcoal this must now be inked in or fixed. I usually prefer a light, sepia ink made from Vandyke crystals boiled in water and used with a little strong glue-size added to ensure fixing. The whole charcoal drawing is then redrawn with a fine fitch in this ink.

The charcoal is removed when the ink is bone-dry by using a flogger as previously described.

When we have decided on the kind of painting to be done, and the strength of the size to be used, and the foundation drawing is fixed and certain, we commence painting. I call this the moment of attack: the problems of the drawing and the kind of painting desired have been worked out, and now the painting should be lively — not tentative or laboured. If you are sure that the construction underneath is true, you will be able to achieve a free and confident painting technique. To discover faults at this stage can lead only to disaster.

For theatrical scenery which will be seen from a distance of at least thirty feet (and usually much more) the important thing is vitality of texture. Painting suitable for a shop window would look thin and stilted on stage.

The way one holds a brush is, of course, a personal thing, but a firm intention must underlie its every action. The brush should be loaded with paint, and the brush stroke should end when the paint (or intention) is finished. No matter how trivial it may seem, every mark on the canvas must be clear in its intention, otherwise it becomes woolly-minded and indecisive.

Once the whole surface has been laid into its basic colours and tones, the textures begin to build up. Colour is best applied separately, like pointillism, as dots or

splashes, allowing the primary colours to lay side by side. This is better than relying too much upon mixes, which tend to look dead and muddy.

The scale of scene-painting from the model is usually $\frac{1}{2}''$ to $1'$. An enlargement by twenty-four times calls for large thinking and action in painting; it is not just a matter of what you see in front of you, but of understanding what is above and below you. Every 'statement' must contribute to the whole effect.

If a mistake is made — for instance, if the colour or tone is found to be wrong after you have commenced painting — do not stop the work, but carry out your original intention. Then you can treat the problem as a whole, and not break the rhythm and continuity.

I do not want to touch upon the content or style of painting, as this is a personal and individually sensitive matter. But whatever the artistic intention, it has to be

Hand splashing.

remembered that painting is an art that must be founded on good craftsmanship. Throughout the whole work on stage there must be a sense of continuity and a feeling of major movement.

I shall take an example and describe the various stages of its development — namely, the dropcloth to *The Italian Straw Hat* produced at the Old Vic in 1951 and designed by Roger Furze. The design was unusual, in that it was executed in oils. The scale was approximately 1″ to 1′.

I first carefully lined the major statement of the picture in charcoal, the horizontal lines suggesting street architecture, the mass shapes depicting tree foliage and sunlit passages.

Into this I sketched at the same time the life in the street: people, horses, carriages. In all of this I was concerned with the relations and the infrastructure of objects, which made the movement of the whole. Examples were the architectural spaces in between windows and archways; the ratio in mass of one building to another.

The people were sketched in the nude so that I could understand them anatomically.

(Opposite top) The *Italian Straw Hat* at the Old Vic (1951). Designer: Roger Furze. Director: Denis Carey.

(Opposite bottom) The cloth for the *Italian Straw Hat*. Compare this with the original design.

The Italian Straw Hat: a simulation of the actual painting which illustrates the scale of the model to the cloth.

THE ART OF SCENE PAINTING

When this first stage was finished I had a lively sketch of the whole thing, but without its detail and decoration. I was then able with a brush, in a Vandyke or sepia ink, to develop and embellish the whole scene, in both the animate and the inanimate content of the design.

Then in light and shade I had to suggest the thick (impasto) of the brush strokes. This was achieved by using the size medium cold as a jelly, which gives the appearance of a thick texture. I painted on a 'scumbled' white surface with both glaze and opaque paints, working from dark to light, as in oil painting.

I now had a sepia drawing free and interesting, based on the truth. Because I could understand the structure of the architecture I could apply the brush strokes suggesting stone, etc., and by understanding the anatomy of the people in the work I could clothe and drape them correctly.

I worked throughout in stages, not carrying any part of the painting ahead of the whole conception at any time. Consequently, the work always had a complete look. In fact, I was never able to put the final dark tones in, but the cloth did not look unfinished.

Architecture

Here are a few hints on the realistic painting of architecture, to give the illusion of three dimensions.

The drawing of architectural scenery needs a great deal of special study, as does the understanding of stage perspective. I shall give a few simple hints on perspective later.

The realistic painting of architectural features — for example, columns and capitals — can give the impression of three dimensions if the colour and tone of the shadows and lights are carefully chosen to relate to the ground colour. Usually the tone of shadow is about the same as the ground colour when wet.

If the ground colour is made darker by the addition of black, a tiny amount of rich colour must be added or the shadow will look dead and false. I follow the old adage, highlights thick and shadows thin, keeping the shadow-colour translucent to enable the form underneath to 'grin through', thereby making the shadow-area look alive and rich.

Keep the shadow very simple: one or two tones should be sufficient, lights and half-lights.

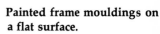

Painted frame mouldings on a flat surface.

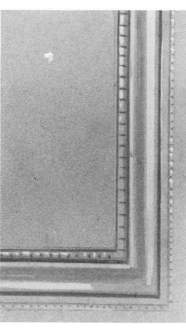

The straight edge. This should be held firmly (but not stiffly) at the point of balance.

Again the rule is simplicity, and if whiting (chalk) is used to lighten the ground a richer pigment must be added, otherwise the colour will look chalky and weak. In the case of highlights it is sometimes advantageous to leave the point of light as pure white paint and glaze a tint on it when it is dry.

The ruling of moulding with a straight edge is a matter of practice. It is merely a trick, and can be mastered fairly easily.

If possible it is good to set the direction of the light source.

Every mark made must be full of intention. If the drawn line is tight and without the confidence that comes from authority there will be no freedom or vitality in the work.

In the setting out of mouldings, a chalk-line and straight edge are used.

The straight edge should be held firmly but not stiffly at the point of balance, and the brush lightly drawn along the edge, giving a thin, sensitive line.

The chalk-line is used to snap clean the charcoal lines between points.

It must be remembered that all scene-painting is enlargement. It is most important to magnify the texture of the work, and every aspect has texture. If, for instance, the original model has a very textured surface, then an enlargement of this must be applied to the whole surface.

I find that it is better to use the edge of a large brush to execute even a fine line rather than the point of a fitch or small lines expressed by the point of a brush. These have no texture or freedom and tend to tighten the appearance of the drawing, making it seem hard and wiry like a steel engraving.

The use of the straight edge in the painting of a straight line.

THE ART OF SCENE PAINTING

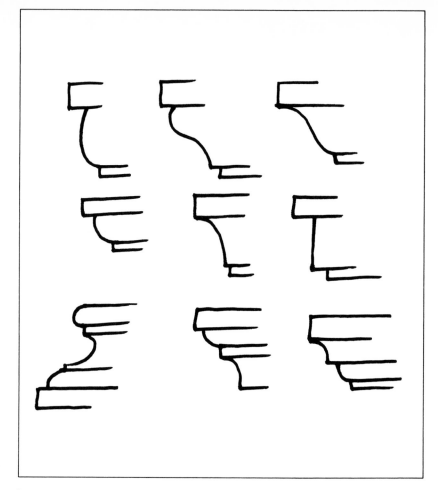

A section of simple mouldings.

All drawing must be of good proportion, with all sections of details, moulding, etc., based on the classical rules of the period concerned. Any form of fussy detail or sectional form without authority will be seen in the finished work, and ruin the major statement.

Any treatment to suggest antiquity must be part of the under-painting and not superimposed with a spray as an after-thought, which would become immediately obvious.

In general, a light, free handling of the brush is to be preferred to a tightly controlled and stiff operation. Colour should always be thin and flowing, rather than thick and pudding-like.

Brushes should be suspended in water when not in use and washed in cold water, as hot water spreads the bristles.

Painting

The large masses of colour and broadness of brushwork seem to suggest that scene-painting is a somewhat slap-dash business. This is only true of work that is without intention and thought, when the broadness is roughness (and so has no vitality) and the large colour masses have no variation or intended texture.

As I see it, the task of the brush is to apply paint as either a flat mass or a broken texture. In all forms of materials there is texture, and as one is enlarging up so the texture also grows. For example, if a design was made on rough paper then I would cover the whole cloth with a similar texture on the drawing.

I never use the point of a brush, as this is thin and characterless, whereas the side of a brush will leave a textured mark or line similar to the magnified original line.

The approach to the painting to be done depends a great deal on the original design and on the plan of attack and translation intended.

The use of the side of the brush in order to create texture.

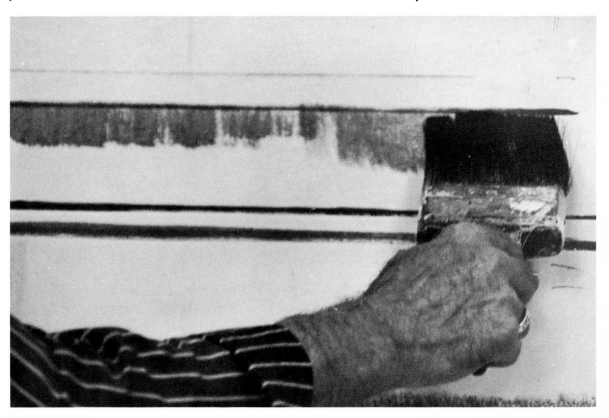

THE ART OF SCENE PAINTING

Generally the major techniques can be divided as follows, but it must be remembered that these can be skilfully mixed, and overlapped to give vitality and energy to the work.

Opaque painting

Colours mixed in pots. Basically light on dark.

The opaque technique is mostly useful for design· in poster style and flat masses.

It is most essential that even when opacity is desired the paint should not be too thick or pudding-like if the cloth is to roll up. It is only necessary to load sufficient pigment to reach the degree of opacity required, and this also enables the drawing underneath to grin through.

Owing to the chalky nature of most scenic colours, the additional opaque layers tend to appear much lighter and whiter in tone, giving an overall chalky pastel appearance to the work.

Once you have decided on the kind of treatment the cloth requires, the next question is the strength of the size-medium to be used throughout the work. This depends on the kind of paint required; if opaque the size must be strong enough to fix the amount of pigment and whiting in the mixture, but not strong enough to crack or pucker the cloth. Four parts water to one of size should be sufficient to hold a reasonably solid opaque paint, but a weaker size would be better if it can fix the pigment. Two thin coats are always better than one thick coat.

Glaze painting

This is modelling drawn underneath colour applied in translucent glazes, as in the Italian thirteenth and fourteenth century masters. In transparent glaze-painting the medium should be fairly diluted. If the medium is too strong (whether size or emulsion) the results will be uneven and patchy. Glazes should be applied freely and quickly, so as not to disturb the drawing underneath, and to preserve a fresh quality.

Aniline dyes can be used in this way, but this needs the confidence gained by experience, as they are permanent and cannot be erased.

Doctor Faustus (designer Farrah; producer Clifford Williams): a section of the act-drop, after Hieronymus Bosch.

The Roaring Girl **(producer Barry Kyle; designer Chris Dyer). The screen of Eliza-bethan dignitaries was embell-ished in gold.**

Palette painting

Using both opaque and glaze colours straight from the palette (*alla prima*).

Even in the most simple work I prefer to use the palette. My method is to rely on two or three basic colours and to mix them on it with other colours. This gives greater variety and freedom to the basic lay-in.

The art of palette painting is in being able to judge colour and tone in the wet. When you have achieved the colour that you want you always leave a little on the palette to compare it with the next mix.

For speed and freedom of work it is advisable to have a large container of medium size or PVA (polyvinyl acetate) and a bucket of water by the palette to keep the washes of colour clean and free, and of course to change them for fresh when they get muddy. In the painting of large cloths it is essential to have plenty of all materials available so as not to stop and remix during painting, because this would be disastrous.

Painting on the Floor

A method used almost always on the Continent, where they are geared to it and have travelling bridges and balconies to view the work from. Both methods have their advantages and snags. Large washes and textures are easier and more effective on the floor. The building up of layers of colour, and the use of the great variety of puddles and gradations, is more difficult to achieve on a vertical frame. I have used the floor many times, and learned from the Russian Ballet painters that, as with all good work, one should experiment before starting.

The floor should be smooth, and if possible it is sometimes good to put a clean, smooth backcloth underneath. The cloth should be sized with a fairly light dilution of size or emulsion; about six or even ten parts of water to one of medium. This size depends on the amount of pigment to be

Painting on the floor at the Royal Opera Centre.

fixed and must not be too strong, as it will adhere to the surface underneath. Brushes should be attached to canes, and for architectural work straight edges should also be attached the same way. The length of the canes needed depends on the painter's reach.

My experience is that the floor is easier and faster in free work, where great sweeping strokes can be applied and a fine vigour achieved. The danger is in getting over-slick or facile. In detailed and architectural work the floor is more difficult, but can be mastered.

One or two pairs of step-ladders are needed to get a view of the whole work from above. Polunin, my predecessor at the Slade School of Fine Art, was a great exponent of this art, and together with other Russian painters produced fine works for the Russian Ballet; he also worked on *Tricorne*, where Picasso himself painted the scenery on the floor.

Because of its three-dimensional quality, using plastic and plaster, a great deal of modern scenery has to be done on the floor. The same rules apply; you must think big and keep up the scale, and must view the work from above.

(Opposite top)
Creating a brick wall out of expanded polystyrene, using naked flame. This is very dangerous, as a lethal gas is given off. Nowadays masks are considered essential.

(Opposite bottom)
Painting on the floor.

THE ART OF SCENE PAINTING

Aniline Dyes

Very rich, pure colour used mainly for curtains and clothes to be kept soft. I sometimes use dyes in conjunction with powder pigments as a booster to brighten colours. The dye should always be boiled and never applied too strongly or thickly. The content of dye crystals must be under saturation point or the colour will crystallize.

Aniline dyes cannot be permanently fixed, but for most theatrical purposes they will be sufficiently stable, especially if about a tablespoon of common salt is added for every two gallons.

Troilus and Cressida: **the RSC, 1960 (designer Leslie Hurry; producer Peter Hall). The throne drape is on Japanese silk.**

(Opposite) The backcloth to *As You Like It* **(designer Farrah; painter John Collins). This is in aniline dye upon canvas, and the size is approximately 28′ deep × 30′ wide.**

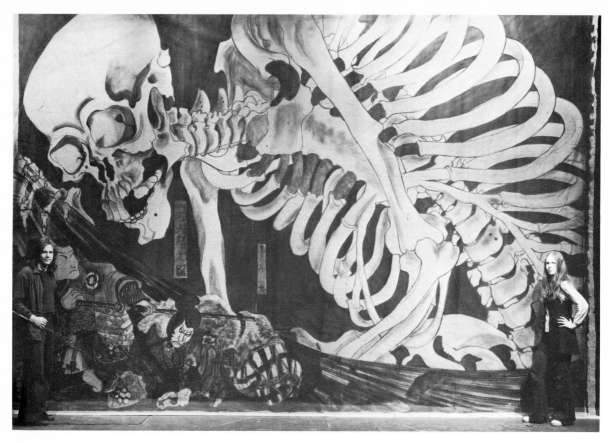

A gauze painted in aniline dye by Slade students Malvern Hostick and Polly Barlow.

As with scene paint (or tempera), it is always advisable to achieve strong colours and tones with aniline dye in thin glazes, rather than in one strong application. Aniline dye should only be used when it is certain that the canvas is not again to be used for painting, as it is impossible completely to obliterate aniline colour. Brushes and hands should be washed in cold water, as heat tends to fix the dye.

When painting dye on plush material it is advisable to use a little flour to lessen the spread of the colour. Sometimes a line painted very finely, in medium-strength size or emulsion-glaze, will help to separate even colours still wet. I usually paint my first layers or washes of dye from bottom to top to avoid drip marks drying in, and of course never stop during the laying in of the whole cloth.

Modern Materials

Plastic emulsion (polyvinyl acetate) used as a medium for scene-painting on canvas.

Priming

I personally prefer glue-size priming, as already described, since it forms a lightly stretched base on which to work, and will tighten up again under another light wash of size. Canvas that has been treated only with emulsion tends to slacken and remain slack.

Medium

As with size, emulsion-glaze is best used in a weak dilution. There is a tendency for emulsion paint to skin and produce a shiny texture if it is applied too thickly. Eight parts of water to one of emulsion should hold most pigment leads. If translucent work is desired twelve parts of water to one is preferable.

Another successful experiment with emulsion was made when certain parts of a gauze had to be solidly filled in. This has always been a problem, because if the paint is thick enough to fill the gauze its size-content is too strong, and causes the gauze to pucker. Emulsion carefully applied does not pucker, and easily fills the netting. I have also used PVA for silk-screen printing described later.

THE ART OF SCENE PAINTING

Other Uses for Emulsion Glaze

Gold Bronze powder

PVA is an ideal medium for fixing metal powder of all descriptions. Normal mixing should be done: always put the powder into the medium, and if water is used it must be cold.

I prefer to employ a method which, although a little more trouble, gives very much better results. The surface is treated with an even coat of PVA, which is allowed almost to dry off; then the metal powder (dry-mixed) is evenly distributed over the surface. I find a metal strainer best for this purpose. When the surface is bone-hard and dry the surplus powder is blown off on to paper and salvaged, and the surface can be gently burnished. This achieves a very bright and metallic finish without the glutinous appearance of the medium over the gold. PVA is an excellent glaze or varnish, achieving an eggshell sheen and drying very quickly.

PVA can be tinted with aniline dye, producing a rich, translucent coloured varnish; the dye must be cold before mixing it with PVA, for the latter is a thermoplastic, and heat will make it into stringy fibres.

Repeating Patterns and Ornaments

The traditional method of repeating or transferring a motif or drawing is by the use of a pounce, which is made by drawing on thick brown or cartridge paper and pricking tiny holes through which a powder colour is rubbed, leaving a dotted line on the surface as a guide to redrawing and painting the motif. This method can be seen in the cartoons of Raphael at the Victoria and Albert Museum. A sharp point such as a dart or large needle should be used, and then it is essential to sandpaper the back of the pounce in order to remove the surplus paper from the holes. The powder colour should suit the colour of the background.

The other method of reproduction is the stencil cut from oiled or waxed paper.

Now, I use various methods based on the principle of silk-screen printing, but not always employing silk; it depends on the size and texture required. I have used various materials, from fine-to wide-mesh gauze. In making the screen the design is left as a defined shape and the background stopped out with shellac or PVA full-strength, in order to remain fixed under the printing process. Printing can be done by spraying or rolling, or by use of a squeegee, whichever suits the purpose best; also it depends on whether you are working vertically or on the flat. I use this method to produce fine effects on carpets; usually the medium is PVA diluted, and either dye or thin scene paint. It is important to test the base carpet to ensure that your colour will adhere to it, as some man-made fibres will not take dye at all.

THE ART OF SCENE PAINTING

Stage Perspective

This is a very specialized subject, and would need a separate study, so I shall only touch upon the basic principles here.

In present-day design perspective is seldom used, but a knowledge of it is useful even in the use of contemporary work. I shall take as my example a classic, architectural one, comprising a backcloth and four wings such as is used in ballet design.

The principle of stage perspective is to give the illusion of greater depth than that of the actual depth of the stage. The size of a human figure has a bearing on stage perspective — more so than in picture perspective. This is because you are dealing with actual size, and on the stage the lower and base perspective is limited to the floor of the stage, whether

A backcloth sketch by the author.

raked or level, and also its relation to the human figure. In general the line of sight is put at about 5′, or eye-level; below this mark all perspective lines level off.

In starting a drawing for stage perspective, the factors are the lines which spring from points on the line of sight; all lines are related to the line of sight. It is best to work out the major statements on paper before attaching the cloth. The drawing and the cloth should be squared up to scale, and the line of sight (LS) set from this line. The points of perspective — which I shall term vanishing points (VP) — should be fixed. There are many tricks contrived to aid the scene-painter in his drawing of perspective, and to help him to project the work from the drawing-board to the large scale of the cloth.

Let us assume the cloth is to be 40′ × 24′. The scale is usually $\frac{1}{2}$″ to 1′, or in today's metric terms some 25–1. Charcoal string-lines are used for putting the lines on the

THE ART OF SCENE PAINTING

Perspective breakdown of a backcloth. VP = Vanishing Point, PC = Perspective Centre.

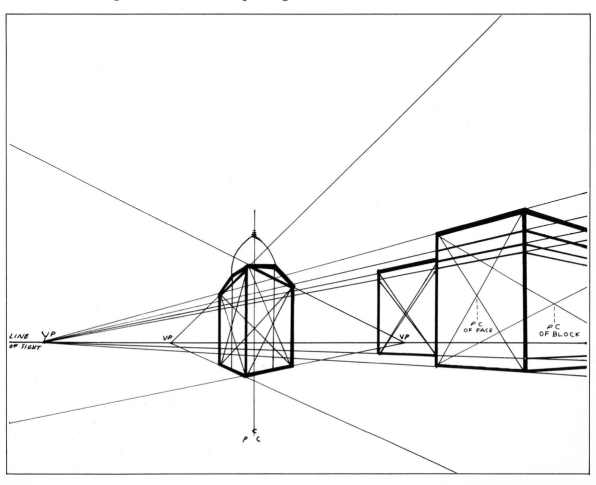

THE ART OF SCENE PAINTING

(Opposite) Carrying the lines
of perspective through
although there is no vanishing
point available. This is done by
marks on the straight edge.
PC = Perspective Centre,
PCB = Perspective Centre of
whole block.

cloth, and a plumb-line is employed to ensure the perpendicular lines are true. Other equipment required for the initial drawing-out includes a straight edge, and safety pins for making points on the canvas, though this can be done with a nail if there is a wood support behind.

I shall concentrate on the basic construction of drawings before I describe the methods used in the final painting. By studying the paintings and drawings of Canaletto, Piranesi and the Bibienna family you will get to understand architectural perspective. This is particularly so in the case of the Bibiennas, who designed a great deal for the theatre and who realized the special requirements for stage perspective.

To begin work on the cloth (assuming it has been prepared for paint or aniline dye), a horizontal line is made along its base, just above the fixing nails; the line must be absolutely level, and to ensure this you should use a spirit-level. You should now decide on the size of the grid to be used, and although I do not always square a cloth, it is best for beginners to do so. I will decide in this work to use a 2' grid. From the base-line strike horizontal lines 2' apart. I begin at the base because it is the foundation of the construction. Having finished the top horizontal line, find the centre and drop a plumb-line, pin the cord to the top batten and when it is steady snap the central, perpendicular line, and the others from the centre outward, both ways. Charcoal must be used very lightly in order to make a clean drawing. The line of sight must now be put in, and the first VP also blocked in. The main structure is then taken off the side walls and interior of the arch. It is important to notice that the vanishing-point for the facing wall is off the cloth, so at this point I will describe the first trick, how to carry the lines of perspective through to their vanishing-point. Although no such point is actually visible, this is done by marking off the lines at the nearest, or foreground, position on to a straight edge, which is then angled at the diminishing end and marked on to the cloth and the line run through. Determine the major perspective lines on the scale drawing first, and then carry out as above on the cloth.

All lines, down to the smallest detail, must originate from the appropriate vanishing-points. As an example of

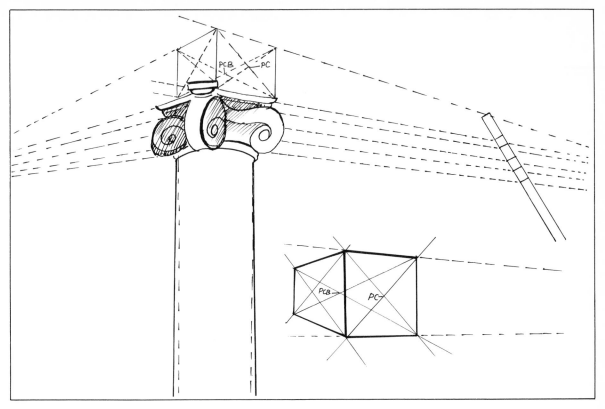

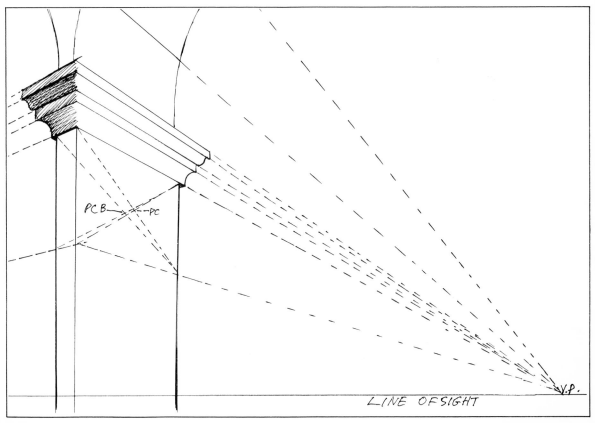

PCB—→ ←—PC

LINE OF SIGHT

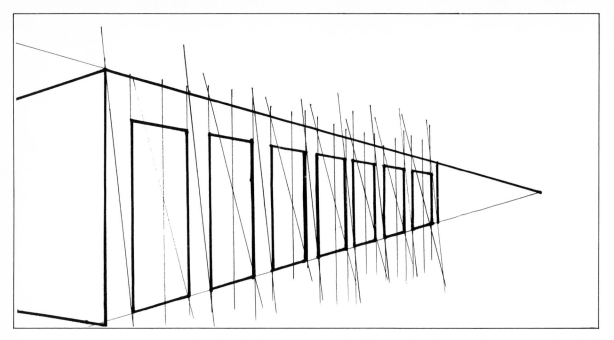

A simple method of using perspective by diminishing lines.

detailed perspective I will use the classic Ionic capital and column. Having established the vanishing-point on the line of sight, it is essential to find the centre of the column and capital. Every detail must have its perspective centre, but once the main lines are in this is not difficult; as I mentioned before, diagrams are better than words on this subject. For drawing a ceiling, and an ellipse or dome, you can use string, straight edge, etc. To transfer simple geometric forms from the drawing-board and magnify by 25–1 is not difficult, if you use the various aids already discussed, and with experience you will gain confidence.

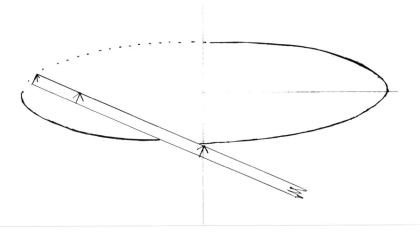

Drawing an ellipse with the aid of a straight edge. Keep both lower marks on the vertical and horizontal lines, ticking points off the top mark.

In painting-in, perspective tonal values are most important, and the understanding of the tone and colour in the foreground, middle and distance tone is more important than colour for realistic scene-painting; but of course this is a matter of personal taste and design, and as I intend to keep off any artistic valuations I shall say that if the cloth is painted in an Impressionist manner pure colour can be most effective. A good painter will use colour like a pointilliste: the pure colour is applied as small brush-strokes or splashed dots, one colour next to another, or one superimposed on the other, sometimes in many layers. This achieves greater clarity and vitality than by mixing the colours together. A cloth painted in this way has vibration and life. A final note on perspective: the scene should be alive, the painting true but free, so as not to have the appearance of an architectural drawing without the human touch.

Materials

Traditional
Flax, linen, canvas bleached or natural, calico (natural), sheeting (bleached), scenic gauze, sharkstooth gauze, filled gauze, hessian, cotton duck, sailcloth, Black Bolton, silk noille, porridge cloth, Jap silk, papier-mâché.

Modern
Plywood. Hardboard, plasterboard. Fibreboard, chipboard, blockboard. Expanded polystyrene. Expanded polyurethane. Fibreglass. Vacuum form plastic. Perspex. Cobex. Aluminium. Copper veneer on paper.

Modern Techniques

Spraying

A very effective and quick method of applying paint or dye or for glazing PVA, not so durable as brushing but good for a smooth, slick finish. Common sense requires the spraying equipment to be kept clean throughout the operation, and a bucket of water kept handy in which to immerse the gun when it is not in use. Most spray guns have adaptable heads to control the shape and angle of spray, and there is normally a tap to control the pressure; low pressure for splatter, high pressure for a fine spray. I prefer splatter for most stage jobs; splatter can be used with pure colours to get a pointillistic effect. The fixative for spraying needs to be stronger than for brushing, and should be tested. The action of spraying should be rhythmic and smooth, not stopping and starting but firing into the air and moving gently on to the surface, otherwise the effect will be spotty and patchy. Very effective spray-work can be achieved by *masking out*, using cut-out shapes of cardboard (or, if working flat, by newspaper and masking tape) and building up the overall picture in sprayed layers. Spraying is a mechanical process, and its success depends on the machine's efficiency.

Texture

Painted texture achieves the illusion of 3D by brushwork marks and splashes, scumble and glazes. 3D texture can be achieved by carving or burning expanded polystyrene or polyurethane or using preformed sections of fibreglass or vacuum form panels. Another way is applying a plaster mix by trowel or by hand. Plaster of Paris, dental plaster and most builder's plasters are too brittle for use on scenery, but are reinforced by adding PVA or glue; however, this is tricky and needs careful experiment on the actual surface to be used. The addition of mica can help to strengthen the mix. Some commercial plasters, Artex and Marbletex, both contain mica and are tough and durable. Another good

Troilus and Cressida: **the back-cloth dye is on a sawdust priming.**

THE ART OF SCENE PAINTING

The texture is wood shavings in plaster (ARTEX).

The texture is plaster (ARTEX) with sawdust glitter and crushed mirror on a metal mesh.

plastic mix is whiting (calcium carbonate, or chalk) mixed with PVA. All the plasters, whether mixed with glue or PVA, must be tested for drying and durability.

The plaster may be loaded with extra materials to give texture — wood sawdust, chippings, shavings, plastic beads, metal swarf, etc. As in mixing powder pigment, the rule with plaster is powder into water, hand-kneaded to a good dough and then spread by trowel or by hand, and if desired further teased out with a stipple brush or smoothed with a trowel.

Carving texture

When the plaster is bone-hard and dry it may be carved in low relief, taking care to wear a mask to avoid inhaling the dust. A very good effect of the terracing pattern on stone — e.g., parings — can be achieved by carving, sanding and polishing.

When carving foam plastics, such as expanded polystyrene, I prefer to cut and carve them cold, without heat, as it gives a sharper look to the work. Tools: saw-edged knives, steel scrapers, etc. Carving with hot knives and wires leaves a soft or moulded look like a chocolate bar or pie-crust. If you do use heat you *must seek expert advice on the correct mask and protective clothing to use, as the vapour given off is LETHAL*.

In order to give a final stony, keen finish I sometimes apply a thin layer of plaster to sharpen the edges and surfaces, especially when the surface has been covered with scrim for strength for touring, etc. The scrim softens the image and looks like pastry, not stone. Expanded polystyrene and polyurethane can be obtained in sheets 8' × 4' thick. They are basically fragile plastics, and need care and protection.

For deep and detailed modelling I prefer fibreglass, which if made well is very strong. When you are treating the surface of fibreglass or vac. form panels you have to break the smooth, sticky plastic look, so you have to experiment with various fixatives such as the spirit mediums button polish, French enamel varnish, white polish (all soluble in methylated spirits), or the resins and polyurethanes. These smooth plastics need to have an abrasive texture for the stage, or they will look bland and

The Jew of Malta **(designer Ralph Koltai; producer Clifford Williams). Expanded polystyrene blocks were dry-carved and surfaced in plaster, then painted.**

(Opposite) *The Jew of Malta.*

paperlike. I have made very effective stained glass for the stage with dyed gauze and linen-framed; I have also used plastic transparent sheet Cobex (motor-bike windscreen) as the base, with crushed Perspex adhered to it to give a deep and textured depth and weight, richly translucent, and colours with resin tints made for colouring fibreglass. The adhesive used was special for Perspex. This was used for Hands and Farrah's *Richard III*. I also treated the great sheets of Perspex for Peter Brook's *Antony and Cleopatra* with dyed PVA sprayed flat on the floor.

Other Effects

Painting the pattern on gauze with clear PVA and sprinkling sawdust on to it is a very effective technique for lighting. It is better to leave the sawdust its natural colour, which varies beautifully in a honey-amber range.

Flock-blowing

A method of laying a light absorbent skin of fluffy dust (flock) on to a fixed surface treated with an adhesive. A box with a crank handle is used to flick the dust. If the surface is painted with PVA it will accept many different substances — glitter (I used crushed mirror), dyed or natural sawdust (see above), sand, mica, coloured glass, beads, sequins; also materials such as silk, scrim, calico, paper, gauze will adhere if ironed on with gentle heat when the PVA is dry. Odd things such as egg-boxes, cartons, shavings, swarf, may be used, but subject to fire regulations.

There are several flame-proofing solutions on the market. Here is a recipe for a do-it-yourself one.

> Borax 10 oz.
> Boracic Acid 8 oz.
> to 1 gallon of water.

Prefabricated latex patterns and mouldings are used a great deal, and need the correct paint to adhere to them. If latex liquid is used in paint and texture you must allow for shrinking.

Repeat Pattern

Methods using pounces, stencils, screens.

Pounces

Select good strong paper. Having drawn the design on the paper, lay it on a cushion of felt or similar fabric, and with a sharp instrument (dart or compass point) prick holes about $\frac{1}{4}''$ to $\frac{1}{2}''$ apart, according to the detail required. When the pricking is finished the paper should be lightly sand-papered on the reverse to remove the ragged paper and make the pounce tidy. The pounce should be marked with bleed-lines to ensure good register. To set out the space for repeating wallpaper patterns, etc., your marks on the flats or cloth must correspond with the bleed-marks on the pounce, stencil or screen. To use the pounce, you rub a powdered colour through the holes, using a cloth pad.

Stencil

This is made of waxed card, or you can contrive one for yourself, using a good strong cartridge paper which you rub with a block of paraffin wax over gentle heat. You place the paper on a smooth metal sheet, applying the wax to both sides until it is translucent. Use a very sharp cutting tool, and remember to place the ties at the vulnerable points to secure the stencil, and finish by making the bleed-marks.

Screens

As in silk-screen printing, the pattern is left open and the background is stopped out. For most scenic work a scenic gauze (a simple open net) is sufficient. For finer work use silk or nylon, although that would be *too* fine for most stage work. Stretch the material on a light but firm wooden frame, draw out the pattern, and lay the frame flat on the bench, raised an inch to clear the bench surface, which is best protected with newspaper. Now stop out the background by painting it to fill completely the holes of the net. PVA polyurethane button polish (shellac) may be used, and sometimes paper can be introduced for rein-forcement. *Make the bleed-marks*.

Pattern on a screen made of gauze, for painting by spraying colour or dye. (One can see students' practice work in the background.)

The reproduction is done by spraying or brushing, and care taken in drying the screen each time. For very simple work the design may be fixed to the screen without stopping out, and repeated by just tracing through with charcoal.

In repeating wallpaper you should use the half-drop method. In all the methods used, make sure that the register on both pattern and background is indicated correctly by the bleed-marks.

Improvising Scenery

The traditional materials for building and painting stage scenery have always been timber canvas and powdered pigment mixed with glue-size as medium. Sometimes because of economy or shortage of materials interesting results can be obtained by improvising with whatever is available. I will take as an example a simple flat to appear as a solid wall. The construction of a flat needs to be from wood: second-hand stuff will do, but metal is unsuitable, whether of tube or angle type, as it is difficult to cover and the frame would be very flimsy.

For normal stage purposes $3'' \times 1''$ timber is used for the main stiles and $2'' \times \frac{7}{8}''$ for toggle rails and braces. The latter should be set back from the face of the flat to allow space between them, and for the material to present adhesion. For many small stages a lighter timber may be used, but it must be strong enough to take the strain and weight of the material when primed and painted, and also light enough to be handled by one or two people. If canvas cannot be used because of economy reasons, cheap coarse material such as hessian, sackcloth, cotton bolton, or anything similar that may be available can be used. The flat should be laid on trestles face side up; this can be done on the floor, but trestles are easier. The material is laid on the face side.

Tack the cloth lightly, starting from corner to corner diagonally and centre to centre, sides and top and bottom. Tacks should be about 2″ apart on the inside edge of the

It is important to set the rails of flats slightly back in order to clear the canvas.

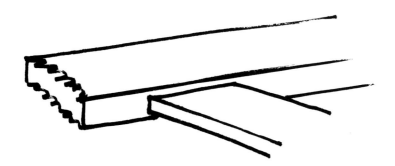

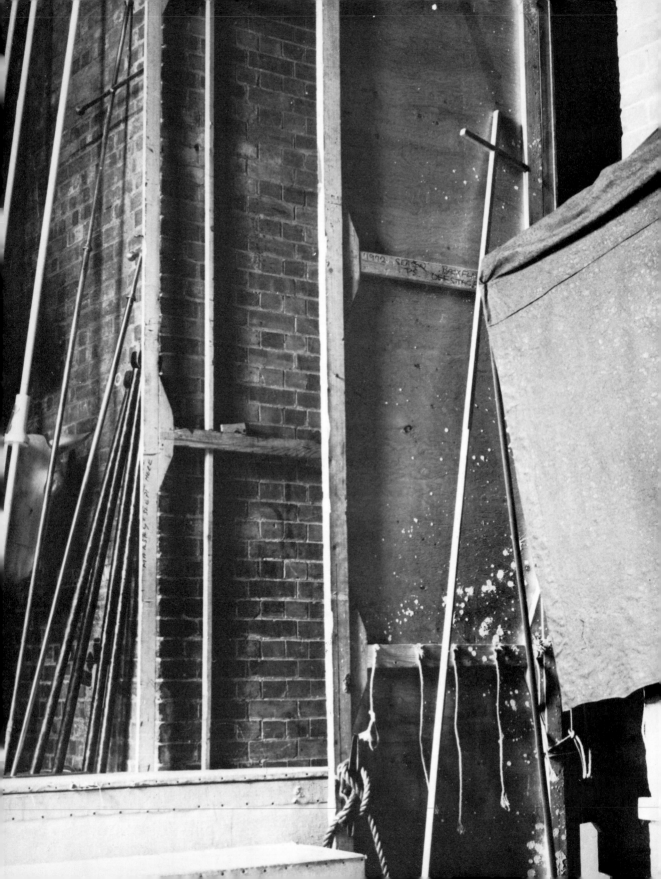

stiles, leaving a flap of canvas to be glued. The glue should be diluted slightly, and the edges of the canvas rubbed down with a wet cloth of hot water. It is important to ensure that the weave of the cloth is not distorted out of square, now the flat is for priming. Although there are many plastic emulsions and PVC glazes available today, I still prefer to use glue-size, mainly because of its capability of being stretched taut again when slack after use. Even if badly dented and slack it can be retightened by the application of water or very light size on the back.

After priming the flat (see p. 19) is ready for the finishing treatment. If a pure painted texture is required this can be achieved by laying the background colour in, and then splattering or rolling a broken texture of various tones of it. Rag rolling can be effective, but all these methods should be tried out first as experiments.

It is important to decide on the strength of size for the whole job: size in the layers above the priming coat must never be stronger than in the coat itself. Top layers can be made of emulsion medium, because although this is more expensive it will stand greater dilution, and does not need heating to dissolve it. Emulsion glaze is sold under many names, but it is usually called transparent emulsion glaze. This can be used in dilution of up to 12 parts of water to 1 glaze, depending on the amount of powder or texture substance it has to support.

Whether you choose emulsion glaze or size medium, the strength you decide on — e.g., 8 water : 1 emulsion — must be constant throughout. Three-dimensional textures need experiment to ensure the medium is sufficiently strong to support them. Cement lightly mixed with 4 – 1, or emulsion 6 – 1, gives a good concrete effect, and can also be washed over with very watery colour. Sawdust mixed with the chosen medium makes a very interesting texture, as do wood chippings and shavings, but they soak up a lot of liquid and take longer to dry. One good method of applying texture is to coat the primed flat with the medium emulsion 4 – 1 or size 3 – 1 and sprinkle sand or sawdust evenly through a large kitchen strainer or sieve — e.g., about 6" in diameter. Paper shredded or crinkled can be used dipped in the medium, but must be coated with a solution of fireproofing mixture.

(Opposite) Backstage at the RSC, showing the back of a flat.

Patterns such as wallpaper can be executed in light relief by painting the pattern or design with the medium and sprinkling the sawdust or sand on while the latter is still wet. It is essential when priming and painting the flat that it should be firmly fixed to the floor or paint frame to avoid warping.

Tips on Economic Ways of Painting Scenery

Still the best and cheapest medium is glue-size (see page 19), which may be used very dilute; for instance, I have diluted 12 or 14 to 1, relying on the build-up of glazes to give me the richness required. Moreover, I would advocate using earth colours, which are cheaper than the lakes and are very beautiful. Use the lakes alone when you have to — this leads to a limited palette, which is a good thing, and is conducive to fine painting. Aniline dyes can be used very economically, and further diluted and used as glazes. The difficulty with dyes is that they cannot be overpainted, and so would not be good for repertory work.

Inventive and Unusual Ideas

Making a stage set of stretched strings (sisal cord) gives a very good lighting construction. Dyed hessian, or scrim used framed and with light passing through, makes a very good base for collage and appliqué. So does gauze or linen scrim, dipped in plaster and modelled or draped and dressed with glitter or broken mirror or sequins, again for lighting. Copper veneer is available backed with a strong paper, and when treated with a solution of ammonium hydrosulphide (smells of rotten eggs) and cleansed with water, it gives a beautiful rainbow-steel colour. Powdered graphite, mixed as a paint with glue-size or PVA and then burnished, gives a very metallic lead look. Wood stained with aniline dye and varnished with PVA gives a lovely wax-like finish. Light-absorption is as important as reflection; for instance, black velvet looks deep and void because its pile absorbs

Hedda Gabler **in working light, the Loft Theatre, Leamington. Director: William Wilkinson; Designer: John Collins.**

THE ART OF SCENE PAINTING

light. I designed a permanent set with the floor made of wood blocks end grain upward and then dyed — it did absorb light, and made a very good neutral surround. Using silver as a base or primer gives a very exciting translucent quality to a set or cloth. Cutting shapes or pattern on a rubber or plastic roller enables patterns and textures to be repeated rapidly.

At the Old Vic I painted cloths and sets in the traditional manner for Roger Furze, James Bailly, Joe Carl, Osbert Lancaster, Leslie Hurry, and in time — slowly but surely — the scenery became more solid and more textured. We had bath loofahs for trees in Cecil Beaton's *Love's Labour's Lost*, great wooden beams for Reece Pemberton's *King Lear*, Kenneth Rowell's collage on gauze for *Hamlet*. The *Electra* for Barbara Hepworth was a great experience. Hepworth produced a model not cardboard and balsa-wood but in plaster, a medium she understood. The set was of truncated columns on a raked base, the fascia of which was inscribed with hieroglyphics. I had the fascia board made of plywood, the marks were cut out and the piece covered with canvas and primed with thick mix of whiting and plaster in size. While it was still wet I pushed a sharp wooden stick into the marks, recreating the sculpture's incision or engraved mark with a soft and a sharp side. I wished to give the whole set a texture enlarging the quality of the plaster 24 – 1, which was the scale we used. However, this was not done, and except for the fascia of the base — which had its plaster texture — the set looked paper-thin. Some wag called it 'Kettle's window', alluding to the cardboard and paper shop.

The art of scene-painting is understanding how to enlarge the picture. This involves not only the texture of background paper, or whatever the model is made of, but also the creation of what is not on the miniature picture; however finely painted the model, there are certain areas which will be thin on the enlargement, and must be fortified by the painter and designer in harmony. A good serious artist, hard-working and capable of fine painting and drawing, will master the art of scene-painting, especially if he or she can work for a master painter.

In the contemporary theatre it is essential that the costumes and properties are part of the whole scene, and

although this is not a scenic job, the painter sometimes finds himself involved. At its best, dyeing and painting of costume is a very fine art by professionals who understand all the methods of the dyeing and printing of fabrics, and it is wise to leave it to them. If the designer wishes to link his costumes and scenery, this may be achieved by splashing or spraying a similar texture (remembering to experiment on samples of the actual costume with thin paint) or dye may be used to break down, or enliven. I must stress the word experiment. So many fabrics will resist paints and dyes, and some mediums will destroy the fabric. Aniline dye is not suitable, as it is difficult to fix and will rub off on to the skin. Very exciting effects can be got by bleaching a design on to a costume, testing the strength of the dilution before starting work. If you use brushes, keep them well washed.

Here are a few ideas and tips for DIY costume painting. Use a fairly dry brush so as not to let the colours bleed, and only a minimum amount of fixative, just enough to hold the colour. For a soft, free-flowing quality, dampen the fabric

THE ART OF SCENE PAINTING

before applying the colour. Printing may be done with blocks made of wood, felt plastic, foam plastic or rubber foam, potato. Simple screen printing can be got from a small frame of silk or nylon organdie net by applying string, paper etc. to the printing face and imprinting with a squeegee; the image will adhere to the screen. You then carry on printing, drying the screen between prints.

The painting of *properties* as costumes is not the job of the scene-painter, but for uniformity in overall appearance is done more and more by him. The process in general is similar to painting scenery. The same rules apply to painting wood, canvas, etc., and the various plastics used need experiment. As the props are handled they must be well fixed so as not to rub. I have painted many portraits and paintings for the stage, and unless they are meant to be theatrical they are best painted straight, in the fine-art style and medium — e.g., oil, tempera, acrylic etc.

I keep in touch with modern materials by visiting building exhibitions and other trade shows in search of ideas and things useful. It is good to look in the material and tool-shops of other professions to find things useful to us. One example is the furrier's knife, a most useful tool.

Nowadays scene-painters' powder pigments are more difficult to obtain than they were — Black Lake and Vandyke Crystals are now virtually unobtainable — but I give a list of suppliers.